Snow Hills, 3rd edition
© 2023, Anna Frazier

All rights reserved. This book or any portion thereof
may not be reproduced or used in any manner whatsoever
without the author's express written permission, except
for the use of quotations in a book review.

Poems
Published 2023
Edited with Carlos Fernandes II

snow hills

ALSO BY ANNA FRAZIER

Elizabeth Young: The Mind's Mess (2020)
The Moon Reaches For Me (2020)
Thank You For The Flowers (2021)
Violet Afternoon (2021)
Adaptations (2022)

View other collections at annafrazierpoetry.com.

snow hills

poems

by Anna Frazier

CONNECT

Visit annafrazierpoetry.com to subscribe to email updates on her new collections, view featured poems, and learn more about the author.

NOTE FROM THE AUTHOR

These books are meant to be read in order as well as from left to right. Welcome to a new space.

DEDICATION

For Hunter Johnson.
You loved me well.

INTRODUCTION

Getting lost in the snowstorm of someone else's lies, of their abuse, makes you forever in a whiteout, and all you can see is the frostbite in your fingers. "Where's the road or home," you think? "Where can I hide from all of it?"

Then someone comes to you through the blizzard and warms your fingers, hands you back the items you lost on the journey, takes you in their arms, and hugs you.

*

This poem series was written during a brief romantic chapter. At its dawn, its end was in sight — it was never intended to last forever.

These poems were written on a Smith Corona Coronet Super 12 typewriter. Each poem's spacing and font are representative of the original poem series as it was first typed. Footnotes will not be included in this collection in order to preserve the original appearance of the series.

The original series was sewn together by hand and gifted to Hunter Johnson.

CONTENTS

BOY AS SNOWSTORM	1
THREE TIMES	2
BOUQUET ON MY DOORSTEP	3
PARACHUTE	4
PINK DAWN	5
PART OF THE DAY	6
LETTER TO MY SEMI-LOVER	7
A SMALL CRYSTAL BELL	8
WHAT DOES HAPPY LOOK LIKE	9
TULIPS	10
EACH FEELING FOR YOU	11
FROST	12
TIE YOUR HOUSE DOWN	13
LETTERS TO GENEVIEVE	14
SILENT LOVE	15
OUT TO SEA	16
HE'S GONE	17
AFTERTHOUGHTS	18
WHEN IT FLOATS AWAY	19
EMPTY	20

SONG
ACKNOWLEDGMENTS
REVIEWS

BOY AS SNOWSTORM

Boy sits next to me on a blue, velvet couch.

His energy is a thick, London fog that calms me down into the cushions.

The wave of his hair is a playground slide. I count the ripples in it — I want to disappear beneath them.

His eyes are shining pennies in the reflection of my pink wine. They glow with the present moment, with "being here now."

Boy's nose is a little hill. The blueprint of his face sends me far out to sea.

While his fingers spin sugar around mine, I want him to untangle me.

His mind seems an atlas, his skin, fresh caramel draped over a soul.

His lips are blown glass stained with Cabernet. He hands me his glass. How close will my lips get to his?

Boy looks into me as I hand the glass back, and his soft touch stops my face from turning toward the windows.

Setting the glass down, he turns my chin to him like a spinning globe, kisses me twice, then stops, brushing my lip corner with his thumb.

His gaze lands on me like a rose petal.

Our movements are stilled in a lovely silence; pause-of-the-world; warm, sleepy air. We are sunset shadows that lean ever closer with each moment's passing.

His presence is the solace felt inside a house as snow falls, quiet, over the roof. He is an afternoon blizzard, silent as a smile, that I lay in, that I am lost in, that I bat away with my eyelashes, catch on my tongue, laugh into, and walk through.

I want to untangle him.

THREE TIMES

I found him, his legs uncrossed in opposing angles,
his hands bright around a glass stem.

*

I ran my finger along the seam of his collarbone,
underneath the neckline of his Indian-red, waffle-
pattern shirt.

*

Since then, little pieces of him have gone everywhere
with me, like dandelion seeds tied to a meadow wind.

BOUQUET ON MY DOORSTEP

He stands sweatered on my doorstep.

His head is a bouquet of tulips.

I'd like to wrap my glass fingers around its base

and lift it right from the ground, out of his shirt,

to my sweetened lips. Each kiss would bloom a flower,

and when I could not carry more blooms, I'd set

him down into his shirt, more lovely than ever before,

and he'd look up at me and smile for having kissed

him at the door.

PARACHUTE

I'm deciding not to be afraid of you

    to lay down in you like a meadow grass

I could attempt to solve our probable end   but

    that would cloud this crystal moment

I'd rather run through the rain   leaving

    my umbrella   red   to decorate the hill

& fly down the curve with my arms for a parachute

    floating straight into you.

PINK DAWN

I roll over and wrap my arms around the just-fallen snow, around a sleeping blade of grass, around a folded rose under my covers.

Do you sleep just so I can wake you? Turn your blossoming head toward my lips so I may crown it with a dozen kisses.

Do you remember my breath as I pour it over your shoulder? Spin so I can empty my hands into yours.

I touch the waves of your arms. I allow my fingers to travel to yours. Let me be the reminders you write on your hands: "Elizabeth," "Elizabeth," "Elizabeth."

PART OF THE DAY

in my mind: i sit by a pond,

    by its water and the wind   sets pink blossoms

in my hair — each minute with you

    takes shape: misty roses

LETTER TO MY SEMI-LOVER

Dear dearest,

    Tu me manques. Do you consider me as often as I walk through fresh-fallen snow? I think, "People like him don't miss people. I feel plagued with a disease you might be incapable of catching — Saudade. My space heater moans on, but I wish she was you. It's five degrees — she can't do what you can. I hear my neighbor wander her wooden floors, and it becomes even harder that I don't hear from you. I'd say I miss you, but then you'd fall into thinking I'll always be here. And, for you, I will be.

                                            Sincerely,

                                            The other half

A SMALL CRYSTAL BELL

let's get lost in happiness
inside a sugarplum   facedown
in a snow angel   let's
take every running moment
that we spend in each other's eyes
and weave them into a needlepoint
pillow   our conversations
are a small crystal bell
let's ring it in the evenings
when the world quiets
when we can finally hear
the other speak

WHAT DOES HAPPY LOOK LIKE

happy looks like a smile   sometimes
laughter a lot   but most of the time
happy looks like a standing girl with a straight face
that's what happy looks like on me   that's when happy
is also tired   happy is not always obvious   happy
looks bored   angry   even sad on me   happy looks
like my pencil moving   my hand holding   my eyes
calming   happy hides in my ribs   in my stomach
lift up my shirt   open my hand   you'll find happiness

when i'm with you   my happy hides too
it veils itself under   my hand in yours   between
the sparks on my cheek   behind my eyes that watch
the snow-covered mountain   on top of my hair as you
weave your magic fingers through it   my happy lives
most often in the space between our bodies when we're
sitting on a blue velvet couch   looking here   there
and at each other   my happy shines in that comfortable
speechlessness   laying my spirit down into bliss

TULIPS

like the tulips
              that rise   in winter
  after years
             of disappearance
 i begin
       to love   again

EACH FEELING FOR YOU

my heart is a window
where blossoms bloom,
each one a feeling for you.

one rose turns to four,
then like fire flies or song notes,
yellow rosebuds on their hedge

overflow the window's ledge.
spilling frills like a yawn,
blooming flowers become a town.

fat, emerald leaves — round
like lace; yellow roses
all over the place.

FROST

i know about
loving someone
who doesn't
love you back

&

i know about
loving someone
who does,
but

what about
someone
who almost does,
who probably will?

my someone
is a slow-forming
frost. i am
a falling temperature,

begging him
to unfurl,
to reach
toward me.

TIE YOUR HOUSE DOWN

if i inhale time
and exhale reality
will it make you stay

if i promise
to fall for you
will you run away

if i trace the outsides
of all ten of your fingers
if i sew a valentine

pattern around the tall stem
of your spine   will you
tie your house down

with ribbons
before it floats
away

LETTERS TO GENEVIEVE

Genevieve,
    What is the point if there's no one to love?
                          Sincerely,
                            Elizabeth

Genevieve,
    I am a heap. I would like to be a heap in his lap.
                          Sincerely,
                            Elizabeth

Genevieve,
    God has asked me not to love him, and I do not know why.
                          Sincerely,
                            Elizabeth

Genevieve,
    I wish I could look at him and cry. I don't think he would understand.
                          Sincerely,
                            Elizabeth

Genevieve,
    I think I know why God has asked me not to love him. Knowing does not help me do it. I must extinguish him, but I don't know how, and that's why I don't know when.
                          Sincerely,
                            Elizabeth

Genevieve,
    I have decided to let our connection kill itself. It has a mind of its own; let's let it do as it sees fit.
                          Sincerely,
                            Elizabeth

SILENT LOVE

we walk through the evening
street. you say it's late,
that you should go. you look at me
for a response. you ask if
i hate you. i stare at the road,
and you stare at me. i don't
hate you; i love you more
than you can know, and i
can never tell you.

i love you even more
than i should, especially
since i shouldn't love you
at all.

i love you, and i told you,
and you said it was nice
to have someone love you,
and i will never tell you again,
because i know you
won't say it back,
and that would be far worse
than the pain of holding back
my words.

OUT TO SEA

you can love someone   for just a little while

& you can love them   when they leave

you can love them differently   in both times

& still escort them   out to sea

HE'S GONE

i fill my house with little yellow roses –
he's gone.

i place a tear on each one, so they sparkle
like his black guitar

under my evening lamp. i sink
into tweed couch cushions

like i used to sink
into his soft brown gaze,

and i wish I'd bought the crystal heart
he picked up at the mineral shop

so i could hold something
he held after he left.

AFTERTHOUGHTS

i didn't know i could love again
after the moon recycled my heart into a sailboat.
i didn't know he had shrunken it too,
and i didn't know it could blossom again either.
i didn't know i couldn't love again
until i began to love you,
until i looked at my lovers before you
and after him & stripped them of their titles.
i didn't know i was loving again
until you were already going.

WHEN IT FLOATS AWAY

i don't resist the sadness.
i am lucky to have been loved,
to have love another soul.
i am gifted with a balloon-
bouquet of beautiful memories:
laughter; frowns; silent, heavy
glances; and more than anything
else, the many smiles we passed
like notes between each other,
each one filled with sugar.

i miss something that is gone,
that was gone before it was here,
that was barely here, that will
always be gone. my body is tight
with emotions. my sweatshirt arms
can't decide which way to cross.
after being closed to the world
for a moment, my eyes open
to a soft, peach sunset. i tie
my wrists down with ribbons,
and my ankles. i sew a kind
pattern around my own spine.
if i promise to fall in love
with myself, will i run away?

EMPTY

it is a stormy day. drapes bluster
inside my white, wooden house.
i watch them and wish for the ocean.

*

a shy wind walks with me
along a nearby shore, where
shades of indigo are stuffed
between jetty rocks. the wind
lifts an iris, and i lift
the one beside it. purple
evening clouds have sailed in.

*

i am a butterfly caught in moonlight.
the wind's breath, thick as a moth,
brushes my cheek and disappears.
dark eyelashes stamp my wan face
as their ink settles in the valleys
of my skin, crinkled from longing.

*

flat on the barren beach,
i try to capture a blue flower
as it vanishes in wet sand.
four empty turtles move across
the shoreline. i watch them
and wish for the wind.

SONG

Inspired by this book's author, the following song was composed by Hunter Johnson. A recording by the artist can be accessed on the website under the book's product page.

ACKNOWLEDGMENTS

Hunter — Thank you for finding the lost pieces of me in a blizzard and giving them back as a gift. Knowing you is a treasure.

REVIEWS

Leave a review of this collection on
annafrazierpoetry.com in the "contact" section.

Reviews help the author's collection to be viewable by a
wider audience, so others can share the experience that
you have just had reading the collection.

www.ingramcontent.com/pod-product-compliance
Lightning Source LLC
LaVergne TN
LVHW031614060526
838201LV00065B/4839